THE
Common
THREAD

Tracing God's Faithfulness
From Abraham to You

STUDY GUIDE

The Common Thread Study Guide

First Printing 2020

ISBN 13: 978-1-930518-06-3

Library of Congress Cataloging-in-Publication Data is on file at the Library of Congress, Washington, DC.

Cover image by Rebecca Stover.

Then I will make you into a great nation, and I will bless you, and I will make your name great, so that you will exemplify divine blessing. I will bless those who bless you, but the one who treats you lightly I must curse, so that all the families of the earth may receive blessing through you.

Genesis 12:2–3

HOW TO USE

We're glad you've chosen to join us for our study The Common Thread: Tracing God's Faithfulness from Abraham to You. This study guide is designed to supplement the video series by engaging your mind and encouraging your heart with additional teaching and activity.

This book is divided into eight sessions—one for each video. Each session begins with a teaser to introduce the video teaching. A longer summary of the session is available on the next page for reference. After watching the video, you'll have a number of brief sections to enhance your learning:

Session Summary
The Land in Focus
Theology in Focus
For the Group
Just for You
For Further Study

You can enjoy this study in a number of ways. Groups might find this helpful as an eight-week Sunday School or small group series, while individuals might use it as a devotional study.

Groups can read The Land in Focus and Theology in Focus sections together before answering the For the Group questions, while the Just for You and For Further Study sections are designed for individuals to complete separately.

Ultimately, this guide is yours to use however you like.

May this study bring you into greater fellowship with God by understanding His faithfulness, His plan for Israel, and the blessings He has given to His Chosen People and the entire world.

THIS BOOK

BACKGROUND

The Land in Focus: The location of each session has deeper biblical significance, which we'll explore in this section.

Theology in Focus: We'll learn a different theological concept to expand upon each session's teaching.

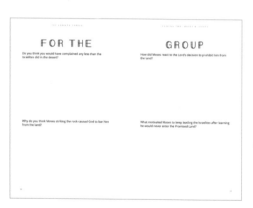

QUESTIONS

For the Group: These questions are meant to encourage group discussion by engaging with the content of each session.

Just for You: You can jump into these questions on your own, as they're intended for personal application and individual reflection.

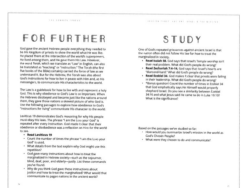

DIGGING DEEPER

For Further Study: This section takes you into Scripture to provide added biblical context while offering questions and activities for independent study.

LEBANON
Dan
Mt. Hermon
Golan
Heights
SYRIA
Capernaum
Haifa
Sea of
Galilee
Cana
Mt. Carmel
Tiberias
Nazareth
Mt. Tabor
Mediterranean Sea
Tel Megiddo
Caesarea
Maritime
Mt. Gilboa
Shechem
Jordan River
Tel Aviv
Jaffa
Bethany
Jericho
Jerusalem
Mt. Nebo
Bethlehem
Dead
Sea
Gaza
Hebron
En Gedi
Masada
JORDAN
EGYPT
Petra
Eilat

SESSION GUIDE

Abraham & Faith

From Genesis to Revelation, one promise of faithfulness ties the Bible together. This common thread starts with God, man, and one step of faith, and it extends throughout the rest of history. Enjoy this session from Tel Dan in Israel introducing Abraham and the eternal significance of his covenant with God for all of humanity.

WATCH SESSION ONE

SESSION SUMMARY

For 75 years Abraham lived in Ur in a family that didn't know the one true God. Instead they followed many pagan gods. Yet God chose to call this man to step out in faith. God called Abraham to leave his land to go to the one prepared for him, and the Lord promised him three things: land, descendants, and a blessing.

Abraham obeyed God's command to leave his land, but as time went by and he and Sarai were not bearing children, he questioned God's promise. But God's faithfulness continued. He affirmed His promise to Abraham, assuring him that he would be blessed with a multitude of offspring.

Abraham believed the Lord, and it was accounted to him as righteousness. His faith serves as a model throughout the rest of the Bible for how people gain favor with God.

Yet Abraham found himself doubting the Lord's promise again, having not yet taken possession of the land he was promised. God made a covenant with him, a common practice in this time 4,000 years ago. The typical procedure was for each person in the covenant to cut up animals for sacrifice and to walk through them together, sealing the covenant. But God walked through alone. He knew Abraham could never keep his end of the covenant with his own faithfulness, so only with God's name is the covenant eternally legitimate because He has never broken His promises.

All families of the earth will be blessed as long as God is the guarantor of the covenant. He wanted to ensure it would be fulfilled so that the whole world would be blessed through His grace, starting with Abraham's one step of faith.

THE LAND IN FOCUS

ABRAHAM'S GATE

When the Mesopotamian kings of modern-day Iran and Iraq came and conquered Sodom and Gomorrah in the Dead Sea valley (c. 2000 BC), Lot was taken captive by their invading armies. Abraham, hearing this, gathered his fighters and pursued the army all the way to "Dan" and rescued his nephew. But "Dan" was the name of the city only after the tribe of Dan conquered it around 600 years later. When Abraham walked through the gates of the city it was either owned by Egyptians or early Canaanites, and called Lashem or Laish. Either way, Abraham very likely walked through the gates shown in this week's session, after chasing the armies for 175 miles and defeating the kings of his former homeland.

THEOLOGY IN FOCUS

THE ABRAHAMIC COVENANT

The Abrahamic Covenant was a series of promises that God made to Abraham to give him a land, descendants, and a special blessing, for him and through him the whole world. In Genesis 12 God promised him many children and that nations would come from him. In Genesis 15, after Abraham moved to the Promised Land and this hadn't yet happened, he had the *chutzpah* to challenge God on keeping His promises. In response God "cut" a covenant with him, a typical kind of treaty in the ancient world between a defeated vassal king and a conquering king. Both would walk through a bloody pool of animals sealing their part in the treaty and symbolizing their death if they didn't adhere to the terms. Notably, Abraham didn't walk through. God walked through twice, making His promises to Abraham unconditional. In Genesis 17 God instituted circumcision as the "sign" of the covenant between Him and Abraham's descendants. God would forever bless those who bless His Chosen People and curse those who curse them.

By faith Abraham obeyed when he was called to go out to a place he would later receive as an inheritance, and he went out without understanding where he was going.

Hebrews 11:8

FOR THE

Why should God's covenant with Abraham mean anything to a Gentile?

Why do you think God was so patient with Abraham in his moments of doubting?

What consequences would exist if God's covenants could be broken?

GROUP

How would this covenant be different if God had chosen to make it with a man who had followed God all his life?

Can you think of other verses/instances in the Bible where faith alone made someone righteous in God's sight?

JUST FOR

Abraham briefly doubted God's promise to provide land in Genesis 15:8. Can you think of a time when you doubted God's ability to provide for you?

When have you been frustrated waiting on God's timing?

YOU

God walked through the cut-up pieces of animals alone when making His covenant with Abraham, who had fallen asleep. When have you tried to "meet God in the pieces" by trying to do what only He can do?

Through Abraham's one step of faith, God promised to redeem the whole world. In which area of your life might God be calling you to take a step of faith?

FOR FURTHER

God promised Abraham three things: land, descendants, and a special blessing that would be for him and the whole world. But the covenant God made with Abraham is a promise that winds its way through the story of the whole Bible. Everything Scripture reveals about history and the gospel is based in the Abrahamic Covenant. Even the covenants that God would make later in Scripture are all an unfolding, or expansion, of aspects of these promises. Use the following passages to explore how God revealed more details over time related to each promise to Abraham.

The Davidic Covenant that God made with David is an expansion of God's promise to Abraham of descendants.
- **Read Genesis 12:1–9 and 2 Samuel 7:17**
- List some of the similarities between these two times God makes promises.
- Because David offered to make God a physical house, God's response was to promise David a "house" (v. 11). List characteristics of the "house" God promised in verses 12–17.
- What do you think it means that Abraham's family (the Davidic dynasty) did not continue to reign in Jerusalem beyond 586 BC. Did God's eternal promise to David and Abraham fail?

STUDY

The Land Covenant that God made with Moses and the Israelites is an expansion of God's promise to Abraham of land.
- **Read Genesis 15:1–20 and Numbers 34:1–15**
- Why does God give such specific boundaries to the land that He's promising?
- Can you identify any of the boundaries on a map?
- What do you think it means that Israel has never yet controlled all the land that God promised?

The New Covenant is an expansion of God's promise to bless Abraham, and through him, the whole world.
- **Read Genesis 12:2–3; 17:1–14** and describe some of the blessings promised to Abraham and his descendants.
- **Read Jeremiah 31:31–37** and describe more blessings God promised to Abraham and his descendants in the New Covenant.
- At the last supper Jesus said that a cup of wine represented His "blood of the covenant." **Read Matthew 26:26–29.** In what ways do the words of Jesus help us understand how the blessings promised to Abraham, and the New Covenant promised to Israel, relate to the whole world?

Moses & Legacy

Have you suffered the pain of never enjoying the reward for your hard work? Moses knew that feeling. Learn why it was necessary for Moses to put his people before himself to continue the common thread of God's grace in this session shot at Mitzpe Jericho.

WATCH SESSION TWO

SESSION SUMMARY

God called Moses to continue the legacy of His covenant with Abraham. Between the lives of these two men, Abraham's descendants had multiplied and became known as the Israelites. God was now ready to call them to the land He promised Abraham.

In Exodus 3 God called Moses to lead His people out of Pharaoh's captivity in Egypt. He indeed used Moses to deliver the Israelites in Exodus 12, yet immediately they began to complain when troubles arose. They were even too afraid to enter the Promised Land! God showed His mercy by providing for the doubting Israelites, but first He caused them to wander for 40 years.

To show His goodness to His people, God allowed Moses to bring forth water from a rock by speaking to it. Because Moses failed to follow God's command, striking the rock instead, God prohibited him from leading the Israelites into the Promised Land.

God led Moses to Mount Nebo, giving him a clear view of the very land into which he was meant to bring his people. He died on that mountain, the border of the Promised Land, just short of reaching the land. He never saw the fulfillment of the ministry to which God had called him.

Moses realized God's promise was not dependent on him or any other man. Only God's name was written on the promise He made to Israel. His faithfulness is what holds His covenant true from generation to generation.

THE LAND IN FOCUS

THE VIEW FROM MOUNT NEBO

Some have proposed that on Mount Nebo God supernaturally allowed Moses to see all of the promised land—and that may be true! However, from Mount Nebo in modern day Jordan, a person can see large portions of the land of Israel. The Dead Sea in the Rift Valley, the lowest place on Earth, is visible from end to end. The Jordan River, Jericho, the Mount of Olives, and even the hills of Bethlehem 50 miles away can all be seen on a clear day. At least portions of the territory given to many of the tribes of Israel are easily visible from Mount Nebo with no supernatural assistance needed.

God's "tour" of Israel for Moses began on the Gilead mountains east of the Jordan Valley running north beyond the Sea of Galilee to the region eventually settled by the tribe of Dan. Then in a counterclockwise motion, God showed Moses portions of Upper and Lower Galilee, bursting with vegetation, followed by the Judean Mountains descending to the coastal plain and the Mediterranean Sea, the Plain of Beersheba, and the Southern Negev desert. After that, God swung Moses' vision back to the region of the Dead Sea, the Rift Valley, and the fertile land northwest of the Dead Sea where the city of Jericho still stands. Imagine having God Himself as your tour guide sweeping you around Eretz Israel! What an overwhelming sight it must have been for desert-weary eyes.

THEOLOGY IN FOCUS

GOD'S STORY OF REDEMPTION

After God punished him for striking the rock, Moses continued to lead the people of Israel. Moses understood he was only a part of what God was doing, a chapter in the larger Story of Redemption. The opening scenes of the story in Scripture promise a better redemption to come. The middle of the story reveals Jesus as the central figure who would accomplish God's final redemption. Unfortunately, that's all many people think about when they say "the story of redemption": humanity's redemption.

But the Bible also promises that God is working many plans and purposes. He's working to redeem His Chosen People, Israel. He's working to redeem His church. He's even working His plan for the angelic hosts. Ultimately, God is working to redeem ALL of His created order that was cursed in the fall to reveal His own glory. The story's closing scenes will include every molecule of creation being set right, giving praise to the Hero of the story, the King of the universe. Moses was one chapter of this story. You are another.

By faith, when he grew up, Moses refused to be called the son of Pharaoh's daughter, choosing rather to be ill-treated with the people of God than to enjoy sin's fleeting pleasure.

Hebrews 11:24–25

FOR THE

Do you think you would have complained any less than the Israelites did in the desert?

Why do you think Moses striking the rock caused God to bar him from the land?

GROUP

How did Moses react to the Lord's decision to prohibit him from the land?

What motivated Moses to keep leading the Israelites after learning he would never enter the Promised Land?

JUST FOR

Moses never saw the fulfillment of God's promise in that he never got to enter the Promised Land. What goals have you worked towards that you may never see finished?

How can you be content if your goals remain unfulfilled in your lifetime?

Moses kept leading the Israelites despite knowing he would never see the fulfillment of God's promise. How does this example of endurance challenge you in your service for God?

YOU

When do you find yourself focusing on your own importance in your work rather than God's plan and how you fit into it?

In your life, how can you work toward "handing the baton" off to the next generation?

FOR FURTHER

Though Moses never saw the completion of the task God gave him, he was an extremely important figure in God's plan to redeem people. He was so important, in fact, that God promised one day He would raise up another prophet "like Moses" to whom Israel must listen (Dt. 18:15–19). Jesus was the fulfillment of that prophecy. The New Testament frequently points out connections between Jesus' ministry and Moses', and careful Bible readers should notice at least three significant similarities. Both Moses and Jesus had

    1) a prophetic ministry of direct communication with God
    2) a covenantal ministry mediating and teaching God's law
    3) a ministry of miracles performed by God's power

Use the following passages to examine the claim that Jesus was the Prophet "like Moses" for whom Israel was waiting.

A prophetic ministry of direct communication with God
- **Read Deuteronomy 18:18–19** and describe the defining characteristic of a prophet according to Moses.
- **Read John 12:49–50 (see also John 8:28; John 14:10).** Why do you think Jesus insisted His teaching came from God, not from Himself?
- **Read Matthew 17:1–8.** List a few ways this passage describes Jesus as a prophet like Moses.

STUDY

A covenantal ministry mediating and teaching God's law
- **Read Deuteronomy 18:15–17** and describe the job God gave to Moses because the people were too afraid to listen to God **(see also Exodus 19).**
- Moses went up onto Mount Sinai to receive the five books of the Law (Torah) from God: Genesis, Exodus, Leviticus, Numbers, and Deuteronomy. Similarly, Matthew's Gospel includes five of Jesus' major sermons. Most scholars agree that Jesus' teachings in Matthew 5—7; 10; 13; 18; and 23—25 are intended to remind us of the five books of the Torah. Scan these five discourses by Jesus and create a sermon title for each of these five "sermons."
- **Read Hebrews 8** and list at least three ways that the New Covenant which Jesus mediates is better than the Mosaic Covenant Moses mediated. Include your reasoning.

A ministry of miracles performed by God's power
- **Read Exodus 16:1–12, 31–36** and explain why in your opinion the miracle of manna was so significant in Moses' ministry.
- In John 6, Jesus miraculously fed 5,000 people, after which many Jews believed that Jesus was "indeed the Prophet who is to come into the world" (v. 14). This is a reference to Deuteronomy 18:18. But then Jesus pointed out significant differences between Moses' miracle of bread and His. **Read John 6:25–51** and list some of those differences.
- Why do you think it is important for New Testament authors to prove to the reader Jesus was the Prophet promised in Deuteronomy 18:18?

40

Ancient Israel & the Mission

Real estate rule #1: Location, location, location! God blessed the descendants of Abraham with the land of Israel, whose central location was part of God's plan for His people to reach all nations. This session from Tel Meggido, the gateway to the entire world, explains how Israel's divine role was to become a kingdom of priests, standing between God and humanity.

WATCH SESSION THREE

41

SESSION SUMMARY

We're focusing not on a man of Israel but the land of Israel this session—specifically Tel Megiddo, a land for which armies have fought for thousands of years. Its importance will last until the end of days, as the final battle of Armageddon will take place in this very land. Why is it so coveted? Simple: its location. It's essentially the center of the world, as it connects Asia, Africa, and Europe. All civilizations passed through Tel Megiddo to conduct business and exchange ideas in the ancient world.

God chose this land for His people for a very important reason. If they controlled Megiddo, they could access the entire world without ever leaving their own land. Rather than sending His people throughout the whole world, God brought the world to Israel's doorstep. To accomplish His purpose, God wanted His people to fulfill their special role: a kingdom of priests. As priests stand between God and man and bring the people into His worship, God wanted Israel to bring people from all over the world to the knowledge of His goodness.

Rather than influencing others, Israel became influenced by sinful cultures that deteriorated their relationship with God. Israel introduced false idols in the Temple, a betrayal of God in the place where only He should be worshiped. By losing this spiritual battle, Israel could not display His character to the rest of the world. The Israelites needed to obey God before they could fulfill their role as a kingdom of priests.

THE LAND IN FOCUS

THE INTERNATIONAL TRUNK ROAD

The ancient city of Megiddo was built along an ancient road that archaeologists now call the International Trunk Road. Biblical scholars often refer to it as the *Via Maris*, translated from Latin as "The Way of the Sea," a reference to Isaiah 9:1. This was arguably the most important roadway in the ancient world, as it connected Egypt and Africa with Mesopotamia and Asia for trade, cultural exchange, and even war. The road ran from Egypt along the Mediterranean Sea all the way to Northern Israel where it cut through the Jezreel Valley and began its trek through Galilee, up along the foothills of Mount Hermon, all the way to Damascus and the rest of Asia.

God chose to place the land of Israel at the crossroads of the known world, putting God's Chosen People in position to significantly influence world events. The Hebrews had no need to take God to the nations. The nations walked past their front door every day. God knew just where to place the people who were to be marked by His name and character.

THEOLOGY IN FOCUS

KINGDOM OF PRIESTS

Most scholars believe the Mosaic Covenant between God and Israel at Mount Sinai is divided into three major sections.
1. Ceremonial laws (Levitical sacrifices and worship)
2. Civil laws (government)
3. Moral laws (ethics and behavioral practice)

But God gave many laws that don't fit neatly into any of these categories. Some examples include God's commands to wear tassels (*tsitsiyot*), not cut the corners of their hair, and avoid mold. While many of these laws make more sense with a modern understanding of science and healthy living, others still just sound odd. But that might be exactly the point.

When God made Israel His "kingdom of priests" (Ex. 19:6), He made them distinct from every other nation on Earth. Some of the laws God gave may simply have been for the purpose of making them different. Through these laws God dedicated Israel to Himself as a "holy nation" unlike any other. That's how the Hebrew people functioned as a kingdom of priests to the world. They were set apart for God's work to represent Him to all people, just like a priest would. How they lived, what they taught, and what they believed would communicate who God is to the world.

Therefore since we have a great high priest who has passed through the heavens, Jesus the Son of God, let us hold fast to our confession.

Hebrews 4:14

FOR THE

What did God intend by setting Israel apart as a kingdom of priests?

In what ways did Israel fail to exhibit God's character to the nations despite its central location?

GROUP

What does Israel's disobedience to God say about our human nature?

Does Israel's geographic location still matter in modern times?

JUST FOR

When Isael began to look, sound, and act just like the pagan nations of the ancient world, the Israelites failed to fulfill God's purpose for them as a people set apart from the rest of the world. Do you ever struggle to be different from the world? Do you have trouble knowing how to be a part of the world while avoiding worldliness?

God purposely places people right where they are to fulfill a calling. In what ways can you serve the Lord right where you are?

YOU

When you are obedient to God, you live out His character to those around you. How would your life look different if you kept this in mind at all times?

What helps you maintain a heart of worship for God?

How have you drawn closer to God during the rocky parts of your spiritual relationship with Him?

FOR FURTHER

God gave the ancient Hebrew people everything they needed to be His kingdom of priests to show the world what He was like. He placed them at the intersection of the world's superpowers, He lived among them, and He gave them His Law. However, the word *Torah*, which we translate as "Law" in English, can also be translated as "teaching" or "instruction." The Torah (the first five books of the Bible) certainly carried the force of law as we understand it. But for the Hebrew, the Torah was also about God's instructions for how to live in peace with Him and, as His messengers, to communicate His characteristics to the world.

The Law is a guidebook for how to live with and represent a holy God. This is why obedience to God's Law is so important. When the Hebrews disobeyed and became just like the nations around them, they gave those nations a skewed picture of who God is. Use the following passages to explore how obedience to God's "instructions for living" communicate His character to the world.

Leviticus 19 demonstrates God's reasoning for why His people must obey His laws. The phrase "I am the LORD your God" is repeated after every instruction. God made it clear that their obedience or disobedience was a reflection on Him for the world to see.

- **Read Leviticus 19**
- Count the number of times the phrase "I am the LORD your God" is used.
- What details from the text explain why God might use this repetition?
- God gave many instructions about how to treat the marginalized in Hebrew society—such as the sojourner, blind, deaf, poor, and elderly—justly. List these commands you've found.
- Why do you think God gave these instructions about justice and how to treat the marginalized? What would that communicate to pagan nations in the ancient world?

SESSION THREE: ANCIENT ISRAEL & THE MISSION

STUDY

One of God's repeated grievances against ancient Israel is that the nation often did not follow His law for how to treat the marginalized in society.

- **Read Isaiah 58.** God says that Israel's Temple worship isn't their real problem. What did God's people do wrong?
- **Read Zechariah 7:4–14.** God says that Israel's hearts are "diamond-hard." What did God's people do wrong?
- **Read Ezekiel 34.** God makes it clear that priests were failing in their leadership. What did God's people do wrong?
- *Bonus question! Count the number of times in Ezekiel 34 that God emphatically says He Himself would properly shepherd Israel. Do you see a similarity between Ezekiel 34:16 and what Jesus said He came to do in Luke 19:10? What is the significance?

Based on the passages we've studied so far:
- How would you summarize Israel's mission in the world as God's Chosen People?
- What were they chosen to do and communicate?

Prophets & Judgment

In the days of Elijah, Israel was a spiritual mess. Division, famine, and pagan worship ruled the land and sent Israel down a path of ruin. Yet in these darkest moments, God still offered hope. Let's take a bird's-eye view at Israel high atop Mount Carmel in this session as we examine the dual responsibilities of the prophets to preach judgment and hope to the people.

WATCH SESSION FOUR

SESSION SUMMARY

One of the best-known Old Testament promises of God is found in Jeremiah 29:11. It's a favorite verse for many, one that gives confidence and hope in the Lord. But when Israel first received these words, its circumstances were anything but hopeful.

Let's start back in the time of Elijah. In those days Israel was nothing like the kingdom of priests God intended for it to be. Pagan worship and famine ravaged the divided kingdoms of the Holy Land. Elijah confronted Israel's King Ahab, telling him the famine was a result of Ahab's willingness to serve false gods in defiance before the one true God.

Elijah, of course, was right. In Deuteronomy 8 while Moses still led the Israelites, God affirmed His covenant with His Chosen People, promising great blessings if they would obey Him but judgment if they disobeyed and served other gods. So God had stopped the rain, causing a drought and famine in response to Israel's disobedience.

It wouldn't be long before He brought other nations into the Holy Land, scattering the Israelites throughout the earth and exiling them from the land. The Babylonian and Assyrian captivities in 722 and 586 BC drove them from the land of Israel completely. All hope seemed lost.

This is where Jeremiah comes in. The prophet's responsibility was to judge Israel according to the Law as its people lived in sin. But that didn't mean he couldn't give them hope for the future. So he wrote of the plans the Lord had for His people, plans to prosper them, not to harm them. God has been, is, and always will be the God of second chances whose promises never fail and whose covenants will not be broken.

THE LAND IN FOCUS

MOUNT CARMEL

The physical features of Mount Carmel contributed to the rigorous day Elijah had when he challenged the prophets of Baal in 1 Kings 18. Elijah climbed the mountain from the steep eastern slopes to make his challenge, bringing the bull for sacrifice with him. When the prayers of the prophets of Baal went unanswered, Elijah built an altar by himself on top of the mountain, butchered the bull for sacrifice, and prayed for God to answer with fire to consume the sacrifice, which God did. Then Elijah ordered the prophets to be captured. He brought all 450 of them down the mountain to the brook of Kishon—approximately a 3.5-mile hike. There he slaughtered them all.

Elijah hiked back up the mountain where he prayed and watched for rain with his servant. When he saw a cloud, Elijah warned Ahab to leave by chariot, hiked back down the mountain, then essentially ran a marathon ahead of Ahab's chariot, more than 20 miles to the capital city. He may have hiked and run more than 30 miles that day on top of all his other work! Elijah's intense passion for God is worthy of our emulation as we grow to follow and become more like Christ.

THEOLOGY IN FOCUS

SANCTIFICATION

The word *sanctification* means "made holy," or "set apart" for God. The Bible describes three different ways in which the believer is sanctified:

Positional Sanctification is the way in which God made us holy in His sight the day we accepted Jesus as our Savior. (Eph 4:1; 1 Cor. 6:11)

Progressive Sanctification describes the work of the Holy Spirit in us as He conforms us to the image of Jesus by our obedience. (Phil. 2:12–13; Rom. 8:29; 1 Th. 4:3–8)

Ultimate Sanctification is a term that describes how holy we will be on the day we finally enter God's presence. (1 Jn. 3:2–3; Phil. 3:12; Rom. 8:29–30)

Philippians 1:6 says, "He who began a good work in you will be faithful to complete it." God promises He will finish sanctifying us even if our growth is uneven or full of setbacks. The certainty of the promise rests on the bedrock truth that God is always faithful to His people. He doesn't give up on those He has chosen. This is true for Christians, and it's also true with Israel: God isn't finished with us yet! His plans and His promise to His people don't change.

For I am sure of this very thing, that the one who began a good work in you will perfect it until the day of Christ Jesus.

Philippians 1:6

FOR THE

Why do you think people believe sin would cause God to break His covenants with man?

How does God's promise to always keep His covenants reveal His character?

GROUP

What parallels do you see between the process of sanctification and Israel's relationship with God?

Do you think the Israelites realized the magnitude of the warnings for their disobedience? What parallels do you see between the Israelites and believers today?

JUST FOR

Have you ever felt like God might stop loving you when you hit rock bottom in your relationship with Him?

Do you think you would have been more faithful to the Lord if you were in the position of the Israelites?

Y O U

Are you trusting that God will complete a good work in you (Phil. 1:6)?

Despite all of Israel's sin in the Bible, God never breaks His promises. As a believer, what promises from Scripture have you found God to have faithfully held for you?

FOR FURTHER

As Israel fell into disobedience to God, the prophets called Israel to return to God but were largely ignored. God's covenant with Israel seemed to be unraveling as Israel suffered all the curses prescribed in the Mosaic Covenant (Dt. 28). In 722 BC the Assyrians destroyed the northern kingdom of Israel, and in 586 BC the Babylonians destroyed the southern kingdom of Judah. The Hebrew people were scattered. Then it happened again. In AD 70 they were exiled from Jerusalem after its destruction by the Romans. In AD 132 Caesar decreed no Jew could live in Israel because of their revolts. In their darkest days it looked as if maybe God was judging and forsaking Abraham's descendants.

But that's not who God is. God never gives up on His people, even in judgment, and His plans for Israel are not finished. Explore some prophecies to see that God's not done with Israel, just like He's not done with you and me.

God's faithfulness guarantees Israel's future:
- **Read Exodus 34:4–10**
- In this passage God declared His name, part of which was *hesed*, the Hebrew word for covenant-keeping, steadfast love. How does God's character in these verses foreshadow His relationship with Israel?
- **Read Ezekiel 36:16–38**
- In this passage God promised Israel that He planned to bring them back to the land for His own sake. List what God claims this would say to the nations.

STUDY

God plans a literal, physical fulfillment of prophecy:
- **Read Amos 9:8–15**
- Some Christians argue that God's promises to Abraham are now fulfilled spiritually in the church through Jesus. However, Israel was clearly supposed to believe these prophetic promises of a future Kingdom would actually happen. List at least five parts that show the fulfilment will be physical, not a metaphor.

God has plans for Israel that are clearly still in the future:
- After God promised to return Israel to the land in Ezekiel 36, He illustrated their return with the vision in the valley of dry bones, symbolizing their physical, then spiritual rebirth (Ezek. 37:1–14).
- **Read Ezekiel 37:21–28** for the hopeful prophecy that accompanies the vision.
- List five reasons these events must still be in the future today.
- In Romans 11:1 Paul declared God has not rejected Israel; rather He has plans for them. **Read Romans 11:25–29** and for each verse list one proof that God still has future plans for Israel.

SESSION
SUMMARY

The New Covenant & Anticipation

We spend so much of our lives waiting for something to satisfy us. Under Roman oppression, Israel waited for a conqueror to rescue them. In this session from the Sea of Galilee, we'll learn why Jesus' life, death, and resurrection were the fulfillment of the Abrahamic Covenant—even if they didn't meet Israel's expectations for deliverance.

WATCH SESSION FIVE

SESSION SUMMARY

We're diving into the Sea of Galilee in this session. Most of Jesus' ministry took place in this area. His ministry 2,000 years ago is intricately tied to the common thread that started 2,000 years before His life on Earth.

With great anticipation, we often look forward to the culmination of God's promises in the future. Zechariah knew something about anticipation when he learned he would have a child in his old age. He saw the birth of his son, John the Baptist, and the birth of Jesus as an act of God in line with His covenant with Abraham.

The only issue was that it didn't seem like God's timing was right. How could He fulfill His promise when Israel was under the heel of Roman rule? Jesus was indeed a fulfillment of God's promise to send the Messiah from the line of David. But His deliverance didn't appear the way the Israelites expected it to appear.

In His ministry Jesus hardly spent any time dealing with Rome. He had not come to conquer their rule and overthrow the political system. He was aiming at the spiritual condition of Israel.

Jeremiah had prophesied about God's promise to address Israel spiritually. The Law itself had become a stumbling block for the Israelites. The New Covenant God promised was focused inward, transferring the Law from stone tablets to their hearts.

Jesus' message was not well received. Israel wanted a conqueror more than a heart change. Yet through His death, Jesus was fulfilling the covenant. Only His blood could cover us, just as only God's name could be written on His unbreakable covenant with Abraham.

THE LAND IN FOCUS

EVANGELICAL TRIANGLE

Jesus' ministry was a landmark event in history. Because of His life, teaching, death, and resurrection, societies and cultures rose and fell; millions came to faith; and our calendars even changed. There's almost no corner of the world that wasn't affected in some way by what Jesus did in the land of Israel 2,000 years ago.

In hindsight, it's hard to believe Jesus' ministry actually happened in a very small space and time. Some scholars estimate that upwards of 75 percent of Jesus' three-year ministry occurred within a few square miles in the northwest corner of the Sea of Galilee. Most of His miracles were performed at Capernaum, Chorazin, and Bethsaida (Mt. 11:20). These neighboring Galilean villages are now called the Evangelical Triangle. Within this small community of fishing towns Jesus taught His best-known sermons, gathered almost all of His disciples, and performed miracle after miracle. Though it was one of the most religiously zealous places in the world, the Evangelical Triangle was a surprisingly small amount of territory on which Jesus focused so much of His ministry. It is incredible that from such a small neighborhood, filled with commonplace fishermen, stonecutters, and farmers, Jesus changed the course of the world for all time. What does that say about His choice of commonplace people like most of us?

THEOLOGY IN FOCUS

THE NEW COVENANT

Several Old Testament prophets envisioned a day when God would make a new covenant with Israel (Jer. 31; Ezek. 36:22–38). But the New Covenant would be unlike the Mosaic covenant; the rules would not be external. Rather, they would be written on the hearts of the people, meaning they would know, follow, and love the Law of God. Israel would receive forgiveness of their sin, and they would live in a restored relationship with God.

God promised a new covenant with the Jewish people at the time when the kingdom of Judah was under attack and about to be destroyed by the Babylonian army. He used the prophets to tell His people that the judgment they faced did not nullify His promises (Dt. 28). Their failure to live up to the stipulations of the Mosaic Covenant didn't change His plan to keep His unconditional promises to Abraham.

Jesus spoke about the New Covenant at the Last Supper. God would regenerate both the Jewish people and Gentiles through the death, burial, and resurrection of the Messiah. That's why Jesus called the cup a representation of His blood, which He was about to shed to ratify the New Covenant (Mt. 26:28). The promises God made to Israel were still alive and well, and Jesus' work of atonement on the cross makes possible the future fulfillment of all God will do for Israel.

I will give you a new heart, and I will put a new spirit within you. I will remove the heart of stone from your body and give you a heart of flesh.

Ezekiel 36:26

FOR THE

Why was Israel not more accepting of Jesus' ministry?

What made the overthrow of Roman rule more important in the Israelites' eyes than personal atonement?

Was Israel justified in their disappointment when Jesus did not crush the Roman authorities? Why or why not?

GROUP

Can you think of other instances in the Bible when someone turned down a greater reward for immediate satisfaction?

How does God's covenant with Abraham compare and contrast with the New Covenant?

JUST FOR

Israel was more concerned with its external enemies than its internal condition. What external issues keep you from spiritual growth?

When have you hoped for relief from your present circumstances more than you have waited patiently on God?

YOU

As believers we eagerly anticipate the day Jesus comes again. But it's easy to lose focus as we wait. What can you do every day to keep your focus on His return?

If you lived in Israel during Jesus' time, do you think you would have believed He was the Messiah? Why or why not?

FOR FURTHER

Have you ever wondered why God doesn't just forgive all sin? The reason lies in the fact that God is holy and completely just, but He is also gracious. This seeming contradiction between God's attributes sets the stage for one of the most wondrous displays of God's greatness: the gospel. By taking the sin of mankind upon Himself in Jesus and punishing it on the cross, exhausting His justice, then graciously applying that atonement to each of us who believe it is enough to save us, God created a way to be both just and the Justifier. The gospel itself is a window into the nature of God.

One way to appreciate the gospel is to trace how the covenants God made with Israel foreshadow and reflect God's redemptive plan through Jesus. There has never been any other way to be saved but by faith. Study these covenants, considering how they point to God's redemptive plan.

A key part of the Abrahamic Covenant and the New Covenant is their methods for atoning for sin.
- **Read Leviticus 4:27–35**
- List the steps a person had to take to make atonement for sin through animal sacrifice under the Mosaic Law.
- None of these steps actually took away sin. The word *atonement* in Hebrew means to "cover" sin, not remove it. Why then did God forgive OT saints' sin (see John 1:29)? Describe how Old Testament saints were "saved."
- **Read Hebrews 10:10–12.**
- How can we know the sacrifice of Jesus' body removes sin?

STUDY

Review the description of the Abrahamic Covenant from Session 1.

- **Read Genesis 15**
- When the ceremony was prepared Abraham fell into a deep sleep. Instead of two kings walking through the animal halves, the text says two symbols, both depicting God, went through the pieces: a clay pot filled with smoking coals and a flaming torch. Can you think of other instances throughout Scripture where God's presence is represented with smoke/ clouds or fire?
- In these ceremonies the animal halves were set on a slight hill so the blood would run together into a bloody pool the participants walked through to symbolize what would happen to them if they broke the covenant. Since God alone walked through the blood, how is this a foreshadowing of Jesus' redemptive work?
- Because God did not allow Abraham to walk between the pieces, He was unconditionally guaranteeing the covenant Himself. Abraham could never keep the terms of the agreement because of his sin. How does this also foreshadow the gospel?

Paul & the Gospel

The common thread is a great blessing to the Jewish people, but what about the Gentiles? Does God promise to bless the whole world or just Israel? This session from Caesarea Maritime shows the extent of God's plan in the Abrahamic Covenant, as we follow Paul's ministry in Rome.

WATCH SESSION SIX

SESSION SUMMARY

When Paul left to be a missionary to the Gentiles, it looked like he was abandoning his Jewish roots. In reality, going to minister to the Gentiles was one of the most Jewish things he could do!

Paul understood that God's promise to Abraham fulfilled through Jesus' rule wasn't limited to Israel, but to all nations of the earth. Paul's job was to convey this fact to the Gentile world. He was determined to explain how Jesus' life, death, burial, resurrection, and ascension into heaven were all tied to the common thread going back to Abraham. God intended to bless not only Israel but the whole world and have all people come to reverence Him. He planned to channel these blessings to the entire world through His chosen nation, Israel.

Following his third missionary journey, Paul sat in jail in Jerusalem for sharing the gospel at the Temple. Miraculously, Jesus appeared to Paul in the prison cell. He told Paul not only would his ministry continue but that it would expand beyond Jerusalem. Jesus was sending him to Rome, the epicenter of the Gentile world, to put the message of hope for all nations in the most influential place on Earth. After patiently waiting in prison in Caesarea for more than two years, Paul sailed into Rome to deliver the Good News of Jesus Christ to Caesar and the Gentile world.

We are blessed to have access to the completed Scriptures because they show us the full extent of God's plan to bless the world. By using Paul to spread the gospel to all people through Rome, God made the common thread clearly visible, a testament to His faithfulness.

THE LAND IN FOCUS

CLASH OF WORLDVIEWS

Throughout Scripture we see a clash of worldviews. The Romans and much of the rest of the world at the time of Christ were Hellenists, influenced by Greek culture, philosophy, and religion. In this society, accolades, status symbols, and power made a person valuable. Most Hebrews, however, saw the world differently. God's Word declared that their worth was based on the fact they were God's creation, bearing His image and called to reveal Him to the world. Most of their buildings were simple, their heroes were elderly instead of beautiful, and honor was reserved for those zealous for God.

In Scripture the apostles encouraged Hellenistic Gentile believers to look to what is unseen, not to what is seen (Heb. 11—12). They admonished them to place their minds on things above (Col. 3:2). They reminded them that our outer bodies are wasting away while God renews our inner person (2 Cor. 4:16). And they declared that pure religion is to take care of those that seemed worthless to an individually-focused Hellenistic culture: orphans, widows, sick, and the elderly (Jas. 1:27).

Caesarea, one of Herod the Great's many engineering marvels, represented the greatest human influence on Earth. But all Herod's buildings are now in ruins. The church is still growing. Take the time to examine where your view of the world and what you consider valuable comes from. We are not of this world.

THEOLOGY IN FOCUS

BLESSING FOR ALL NATIONS

Have you noticed how Jesus liked nicknames? He called Simon "Peter" (little rock), James and John "Sons of Thunder," and Herod Antipas "that fox." Jesus even used nicknames for Himself, veiled references to His own true nature. One name He often used for Himself is "Son of Man." The name comes from Daniel 7:13–14:

> *I saw in the night visions, and behold with the clouds of heaven there came one like a son of man, and he came to the Ancient of Days and was presented before him. And to him was given dominion and glory and a kingdom, that all peoples, nations, and languages should serve him; his dominion is an everlasting dominion which shall not pass away, and his kingdom one that shall not be destroyed.*

In calling Himself the "Son of Man" Jesus referred to His divine nature and His right to judge and rule over every people group, nation, and language. All the Earth will be His Kingdom, all will serve and obey Him, and He'll usher in worldwide peace unlike humanity has ever known. He'll rule the world from Jerusalem, fulfilling all God's promises to Israel and to the whole world from the Abrahamic Covenant and the New Covenant. Paul was a messenger to the Gentiles of this worldwide Good News. The whole world needs to hear what the Messiah has done and is doing for the good of all people.

I heard the voice of the Lord say, "Whom will I send? Who will go on our behalf?" I answered, "Here I am, send me!"

Isaiah 6:8

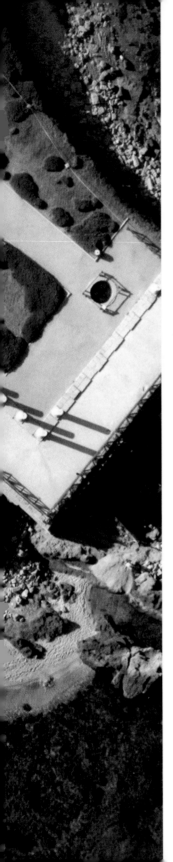

FOR THE

What implications would the common thread have if Gentiles had no access to the blessings of God?

What other verses or passages from the New Testament can you think of that reveal the common thread?

What is the significance of Jesus' Jewish heritage in light of God's covenant with Abraham?

GROUP

What similarities and differences do you see between Abraham and Paul?

Paul took a dangerous risk by telling Caesar, the ruler of Rome, that a greater ruler had come: Jesus, the King of kings. When have you faced a threatening or uncomfortable situation for the sake of evangelism?

JUST FOR

Roman citizenship was an advantage that allowed Paul to escape flogging and continue to proclaim the gospel. What advantages has God given you to better present the gospel?

Paul sat in prison in Caesarea for more than two years. When have you ever felt stuck and unable to make a difference in your own ministry?

YOU

It's difficult to know if God is telling us to change course or persevere in our purposes when trials arise. In Paul's case, years of imprisonment were not a deterrent but a practice in patience. How do you determine whether God is redirecting you or strengthening you when you encounter difficulties?

What experiences can you look back on that demonstrate God's faithfulness during difficult times?

FOR FURTHER

In Acts 26 Paul described the hope of Israel (v. 6) like this: "I stand here testifying both to small and great, saying nothing but what the prophets and Moses said would come to pass: that the Christ [Messiah] must suffer and that, by being the first to rise from the dead, He would proclaim light both to our people and to the Gentiles."

The hope of Israel is that the whole world, first the Jew and then the Gentile, would know God through the Messiah. From the very beginning, the promise God gave to Abraham was ultimately for the good of every tribe, tongue, and nation.

Rewrite each verse below and replace "all nations" (or "people" or "earth") with the name of a different people group (i.e. Swahili, French, Scandinavian, etc). Hear the heartbeat of God and the mission of the gospel.

Example: Genesis 12:3: "I will bless those who bless you, but the one who treats you lightly I must curse, so that <u>Argentinians</u> may receive blessing through you."

Genesis 22:18
Exodus 9:16
Joshua 4:24
1 Kings 8:43
1 Chronicles 16:23–24
Psalm 2:8
Psalm 47:1
Psalm 64:9
Psalm 72:17
Psalm 86:9
Psalm 96:3
Psalm 117:1
Isaiah 2:2
Isaiah 40:5

Isaiah 56:6–7
Isaiah 66:18–19
Daniel 7:14
Zephaniah 3:9
Zechariah 8:23
Matthew 28:19
Mark 13:10
Luke 24:47
Acts 1:8
Galatians 3:8
Philippians 2:10–11
1 Timothy 2:3–4
Revelation 5:9
Revelation 21:23–26

STUDY

Modern Israel & Restoration

God's love story with Israel has lasted thousands of years and will continue forever. We see a testament to His faithfulness in the city of Tel Aviv and the port of Jaffa, our two locations for this session. Watch and learn why it's no mistake that the Jewish people are back in the land that God promised Abraham so long ago.

WATCH SESSION SEVEN

SESSION SUMMARY

This session takes us to Jaffa and Tel Aviv—the old and new landmarks of Israel. In fact, the name Tel Aviv means "the old new city." It's a bustling, thriving, modern-day metropolis, but just outside the city sits the 5,000-year-old port of Jaffa. These two neighboring yet polar opposite locations tell the story of Israel.

The famous author Mark Twain once asked of the Jewish people, "What is the secret of his immortality?" Thanks to Scripture, we know the answer—God and His covenant with Abraham.

It's almost unbelievable the Jewish people have survived for thousands of years. Equally unbelievable is the fact they are back in the land of Israel. But God gave unmistakable proof this would come to pass in Ezekiel 37 when He gave the prophet Ezekiel a vision of dry bones coming to life, which foreshadowed the rebirth of Israel. Nothing can break God's promises. Since His name is on His covenant with Abraham, we are certain He will fulfill the promises of land, descendants, and blessing to Israel forever.

When we look at how easily nations have come and gone throughout history, it is so easy to see God's faithfulness. Powerful people groups like the Assyrians, Babylonians, and Persians all ruled for a time, but their glory was short-lived. Outlasting every civilization in history is the group that has been most targeted for destruction and least likely to survive: the Jewish people. It's all because of God, the One who promised to remain faithful to these people. This God who keeps His promises to Israel is the same God who keeps His promises of faithfulness to all who love Him.

THE LAND IN FOCUS

JAFFA

Jaffa (Joppa) is one of the oldest port cities in the world. In fact, the city is so old some even claim it was founded by Noah's son Japheth. Until the first century BC it was the only port city in Israel, a valuable location in the ancient world.

Around the time Joshua and the Israelites entered the land, Joppa and all the areas along the southern coast of Israel were controlled by the Philistines. The tribe of Dan was given an inheritance that included a portion of this Philistine-controlled area, including the port city of Joppa as its northern border. God placed the tribe here to protect Israel's flanks as its "rear guard," which was their job as far back as the Exodus (Num. 10:25).

However, the tribe of Dan abandoned the land it was called to protect. As evidenced by Samson's story, Dan assimilated into Philistine culture, rather than consistently representing God. Eventually, under Philistine pressure the whole tribe moved north of the sea of Galilee and forfeited its inheritance and calling (Josh. 19:47). The port city of Jaffa and the surrounding area south along the coast remained under Philistine control until David conquered it almost 400 years later. The Philistines remained a thorn in Israel's side for generations. What might have been if Dan had engaged the Philistines as it was commissioned and Jaffa had stayed under Jewish control?

THEOLOGY IN FOCUS

ISRAEL'S MODERN MIRACLE?

After centuries of exile, persecution, and genocide, the Jewish people have returned to the land of Israel. The Bible makes it clear that Israel must be reestablished as a national entity prior to Jesus' return to Earth. In Isaiah 11:10–16 God promised that prior to Jesus' reign He will "extend his hand yet a second time" to miraculously bring back all the remnant of the Jewish people from all over the world. In Amos 9:9–12 God said after He destroyed and scattered Israel, He would later shake Israel out of other nations as with a sieve, and He'd rebuild the nation of Israel and the Davidic throne prior to the Messiah's Kingdom. Daniel prophesied that eventually the Antichrist will make a treaty with Israel that he will later break. Clearly Israel must exist as a nation in order to sign treaties. God's future plans require a Jewish nation to exist.

While we cannot say with certainty that the regathering of Israel today is the regathering described in these texts, the Bible teaches that something much like the modern State of Israel must exist prior to Jesus returning. Are we witnessing the table being set for these prophetic events even now? It seems extremely likely. Either way, God's sovereign, gracious hand is in the events that govern people. Israel's existence is a miracle because God, not people, raises up nations. And He might be preparing Israel for much more.

He will lift a signal flag for the nations; he will gather Israel's dispersed people and assemble Judah's scattered people from the four corners of the earth.

Isaiah 11:12

FOR THE

Is God unable to break His covenants, or does He just choose not to break them?

Do you think the current Jewish autonomy in Israel is permanent, or could they lose control of the land again before Jesus comes back to Earth?

GROUP

Why do many in the church minimize the significance of the modern State of Israel?

Why has God allowed the land of Israel to be controlled by nations other than Israel throughout most of human history?

How would you answer Mark Twain's question: "What is the secret of [Jewish] immortality?"

JUST FOR

What does God's faithfulness to the Jewish people tell you about His character?

God's promises to Israel are evident today. As believers in Jesus, we also enjoy promises from God. Which of His promises are most evident to you?

YOU

Do you ever feel that God has forsaken you when you endure long periods of struggle?

How can you show your appreciation for God's faithfulness in your life?

FOR FURTHER

The existence of the modern State of Israel is an incredible turn of events. What most thought could never, or should ever, happen did happen. The fact that Israel continues to survive threats on every side is a testament not only to Jewish tenacity but God's sovereign hand. However, most of the Jews living in Israel today are secular, not religious. The number of Jews who believe in Messiah Jesus is extremely small; some estimate as few as 20,000–30,000. But Ezekiel tells us this is to be expected. Explore chapters 36—37 to see that God plans for Israel to be regathered as a nation before He spiritually awakens them to Himself.

Scripture speaks about Israel's future return to the land having both physical and spiritual aspects.
- **Read Ezekiel 36**
- Make a chart of two columns, one listing aspects of the physical renewal of the land and Jewish people, and the other listing aspects of the spiritual renewal of the people.

STUDY

The physical and spiritual renewal of Israel will be a two-step process.

- **Read Ezekiel 36:22–24, 32**
- Describe Israel's spiritual condition at the time when God will physically regather the nation.
- The spiritual renewal of Israel after God brings them back to the land is dramatically illustrated by the vision of the valley of dry bones in Ezekiel 37:1–14. The reassembling of dry bones into bodies in verses 1–8 symbolizes Israel's physical regathering. What is the significance of there being no breath in them in v. 8? (See also Ezekiel 36:25–38.)
- When does God say that this final spiritual awakening will take place for Israel (Ezek. 37:15–28)?
- If Israel is currently regathered today, what do you believe this says about the timing of Israel's spiritual awakening?

SESSION SUMMARY

Jesus & the Return

The location of our final stop, the Mount of Olives, represents the hope of all believers. It's the site of Jesus' ascension to heaven and of His future return to Earth. It's here that we'll finally see the culmination of the common thread. Check out this last session to learn why we can look forward to the future and how we should live now.

WATCH SESSION EIGHT

121

SESSION SUMMARY

The Mount of Olives should be a place where believers feel a special connection. It was here from this mountain that Jesus rode a donkey into Jerusalem; and it was here, specifically in the Garden of Gethsemane, that Jesus was led away to be crucified. But most importantly, it's here on the Mount of Olives that Jesus will stand when He comes again.

Isaiah 9:6–7 reveals the future culmination of the common thread reaching back to Abraham. Jesus will rule from Jerusalem with justice and righteousness, bringing peace to the whole world. At this time the descendants of Abraham will be gathered in the land of Israel, and all families of the earth will be blessed. Though only a remnant of Israel now believes in the gospel of Jesus Christ, all of Israel will be saved when Jesus returns to deliver His people.

The salvation of Israel is a big deal. Gentiles have been blessed with the chance to be reconciled to God through Israel's rejection of Jesus the Messiah. But the apostle Paul pointed to greater things when he asked the question, "How much more will their full restoration bring?" Believers want all people to come to know Jesus as their Savior, but the Jewish people's acceptance of Jesus as the Messiah is especially important, as it will bring blessing to the whole world.

What a blessed time that will be! Zechariah 14 reveals that Israel's restoration and Jesus' return will be a joyful time of celebration. The specific holiday we'll celebrate? The Feast of Tabernacles, our reminder of God's provision, protection, and presence. We can live in light of this future glory by staying sober-minded, focused on God and not the world, and by setting our hope on the coming of our Lord and Savior.

THE LAND IN FOCUS

MOUNT OF OLIVES

When Jesus returns to Jerusalem, He'll retrace His own steps. Matthew 21 tells the story of Jesus' "triumphal entry" into Jerusalem on Passover week. On the east slope of the Mount of Olives He raised Lazarus from the dead to show His mastery over resurrection. On the south slope He borrowed a donkey to fulfill the Messianic prophecy of Zechariah 9:9. As He descended the Mount of Olives into Jerusalem, He wept over what might have been if His people had recognized Him. Jesus' entry into Jerusalem ended in a very different kind of triumph than the Jews were expecting. Rather than a coronation, the Passover week ended with sacrifice—the Lamb of God, sacrificed for the sins of the world. He died on Passover, was buried during the Feast of Unleavened Bread, and resurrected on the Feast of First Fruits.

But that walk into Jerusalem was not Jesus' last. He'll walk those steps again when He physically returns to Earth. On the day He destroys armies attacking the Jewish people (Zech. 14; Rev. 19), Jesus will again step foot on the Mount of Olives, splitting it in two and providing a way for His people to escape (Zech. 14:4). Jesus will then ascend His throne in Jerusalem, fulfilling the second half of the prophecy in Zechariah 9:9–10: "He shall speak peace to the nations" and rule "from sea to sea."

THEOLOGY IN FOCUS

PREMILLENNIALISM

It's virtually impossible for Christians to read prophecies like Zechariah 14 and Revelation 19—20 and not get excited about the day Jesus comes back to set up His Kingdom. But there are some who read these prophecies and somehow conclude the reign of the Messiah-King will be in a non-literal, spiritual kingdom that exists before the King actually returns to Earth. Amillennialism (the belief in no physical Messianic Kingdom) explains away prophecies like these with interpretations arguing the prophecies are metaphors and allegories, simply because they don't fit a predefined theological system. The way we read our Bible matters; consistently understanding it as the authors literally intended is important.

The alternative, Premillennialism, consistently interprets the Bible normally and literally, seeing these passages as teaching that the King will come back to Earth before He establishes and rules His literal, physical Kingdom. Revelation says this period will be 1,000 years (*millennium* is from Latin, for 1,000), almost like a "kickoff" party to spending eternity with God. It's during this Millennial Kingdom that all the currently unfulfilled promises God has made to Israel will finally be fully and literally realized, including the promises of the Abrahamic, Davidic, and New Covenants.

On that day his feet will stand on the Mount of Olives that lies to the east of Jerusalem, and the Mount of Olives will be split in half from east to west, leaving a great valley. Half the mountain will move northward and the other half southward.

Zechariah 14:4

FOR THE

Isaiah 9:6–7 says Jesus will promote justice and righteousness when He rules on Earth. How will life under His reign look different than life under the leadership of world leaders today? What problems will be eliminated?

What does Zechariah 14 teach about Israel's future?

GROUP

In our first session we studied how Abraham responded to God's call. What occurred as a result of him living in light of the "how much more?" perspective?

Peter tells us to live sober-mindedly. What does living sober-mindedly in our day and age look like?

JUST FOR

As olives from the Mount of Olives are pressed to make oil, Jesus was pressed and remained obedient to the Father before His arrest and crucifixion. How do you respond when you are pressed in difficult times?

How has the full story of the common thread changed the way you view Scripture?

YOU

What benefits do you recognize in your life that are a direct result of the common thread?

In light of God's promises to Israel yet to be fulfilled, what is your responsibility as a Christian to the Jewish people?

FOR FURTHER

The For Further Study section of Session 1 looked at how each promise in the Abrahamic Covenant was expanded in later covenants. The promises in each of these covenants have aspects that are still unfulfilled. But we know God will fulfill them because it's His name written on the promise. How will God fulfill them? The Millennial Kingdom of Jesus on Earth is when unfulfilled promises God has made to His people will be fulfilled. Examine how this is true with the following passages.

Land:
- **Read Genesis 15:18; Exodus 23:1; and Genesis 17:8**
- On a map or Bible atlas, identify all the (current) countries included in the land God promised Abraham.
- List unfulfilled characteristics of the promise of land in physical and temporal terms.
- Compare them to the description of the boundaries of Israel's land inheritance in the Millennial Kingdom in Ezekiel 47:13–23.

STUDY

Descendants:
- **Read 2 Samuel 7:1-17**
- List unfulfilled characteristics of the promised King (not Solomon) to descend from Abraham and David.
- Compare them to the description of King Jesus in Ezekiel 37:22-28.

Blessing:
- **Read Jeremiah 31:31-37**
- List unfulfilled characteristics of the blessings promised to Israel and the whole world.
- Compare them to the description of the Millennial Kingdom in Isaiah 11-12.

ABOUT THE FRIENDS OF ISRAEL GOSPEL MINISTRY

The Friends of Israel Gospel Ministry (FOI) is a worldwide evangelical ministry proclaiming biblical truth about Israel and the Messiah, while bringing physical and spiritual comfort to the Jewish people.

Established in 1938, FOI was founded as a compassionate effort to meet the spiritual and physical needs of Jewish people whose lives were displaced and tragically affected by the Holocaust.

Today the ministry continues to stand against every form of anti-Semitism, serves Jewish people worldwide, and actively edifies Christians by teaching Scripture that exemplifies why loving the Jewish people and supporting Israel is integral to the Christian faith.

GET CONNECTED

 foi.org   @foigm   @foigm   @foigm   @foigm